NEBRASKA'S FIVE SEASONS

THE BEST OF PAUL FELL

WITH FOREWORD BY ROGER L. WELSCH

J & L Lee Company
P.O. Box 5575
Lincoln, NE 68505

FOREWORD...

Paul Fell makes me very nervous. Oh, he's pleasant enough a fellow, and tells a good story, and puts new batteries in his smoke alarms on New Year's Eve, and flosses regularly and all that, but he still makes me nervous. Take a look at his work on the next hundred pages. See? The man has obviously been spying on me and my family for years, and that makes me nervous.

Apparently Fell has the time and energy to watch us as we watch television, to follow us around the grocery store, to snoop on how we are doing raising our kid, and to spy on me at work. I don't know how he does it, but he manages to sneak around without us knowing and take notes on almost every facet – at least I hope it's *almost* every facet! – of our lives.

And then he has the gall to put all our foibles, habits, goofs, gaffes, and perversities into cartoon form and show them indiscriminately to anyone who wants to join him in his voyeurism. Since you're holding this book in your hands, I suppose you're one of those fellow eavesdroppers and windowpeekers too. For shame!

But you know, I've spent a lot of time looking at American humor and while humor is an elusive and complicated idea, there is one thing for certain about Americans: best of all, we like to laugh at ourselves. In fact, people from all over the world have told me they consider that to be one of America's primary sources of strength – the remarkable ability not to take ourselves too seriously!

And that's what Paul Fell has done for years with his "Sketchbook" series. Oh, I enjoy his editorial cartoons; they are biting, funny, sensitive, and even annoying. (I know, because I was the butt of one of his nastier efforts a few years ago.) But I guess it is the folklorist-anthropologist in me that appreciates Paul's "Sketchbook" panels because Paul has the remarkable capacity to look at the most elusive and peculiar tribe of man we know: us.

And he does it well.

It was maybe seven or eight years ago when Paul included me in one of his editorial cartoons. I called him right away, and I was a little hot. "Look here, Fell," I growled into the telephone. "You got everything wrong. You got me pictured as the big, nasty guy in a tank and you've depicted the rich and powerful clods I am fighting as delicate little pioneers in a covered wagon. Fell, you've libeled me, you have insulted my noble cause, you've encouraged the rascals in this scenario to continue their villainy, and you got everything mixed up. This is outrageous and I want an apology. Oh, by the way, would there be any chance of me getting the original drawing of the cartoon?"

And that's the way it is going to be as you read this collection of the best of Paul's sketchbook. You are going to see yourself at your worst, in the middle of your most desperate crises, up to your noses in trouble of your own making, deluged with disaster, doing thoroughly dumb things.

And you're going to love it.

(Er, by the way, isn't that Paul Fell over there behind that tree? Watching us. Taking notes. Drawing pictures.)

– *Roger Welsch, Dannebrog, Nebraska*

BACKWARD...

The "Sketchbook" feature was born in the summer of 1984 out of a combination of desperation and dumb luck.

For reasons that shall remain forever unclear I was shanghaied into a meeting with the *Lincoln Journal* editors and a big-time consultant from out of town somewhere. The topic of conversation dealt with giving the Saturday newspaper a new "look." As discussion lurched into exciting areas like press deadlines and delivery schedules, my attention span, generally at the level of your average fourth-grader, began to ebb. (Tip to aspiring cartoonists: Always take a sketch pad to crummy, dull meetings. You can doodle to kill time and everyone thinks you're real dedicated, taking notes and all.)

Our publisher, the primary cause of my abduction, began to solicit ideas from the folks seated around the table. An instant before entering an out-of-body state I heard, "and how would you change the Saturday edition, Paul?" Long silence. Eyes boring into me. Nervous perspiration. Suddenly I recalled a weekly cartoon feature that I had enjoyed in my hometown newspaper years ago and "Sketchbook" was in business.

Originally conceived as a humorous look at events around town, the new cartoon panel took on a life and momentum of its own. Like the 600 pound gorilla who sleeps wherever he wants, "Sketchbook" more often than not dictates the direction it wants to go. One week, it's diet tips, the next time holiday preparations, and maybe after that a set of cockeyed directions that make a simple task an experience to be remembered.

"Sketchbook" has been a regular fixture in the Saturday *Lincoln Journal-Star* since those early beginnings. Over the years there has been lots of positive feedback, very few calls to run me out of town, and the satisfaction of knowing that folks look forward to the next opportunity to laugh at themselves via my cartoons. I know that I always look forward to discovering what the next installment of "Sketchbook" will decide it wants to be.

PaulFell "

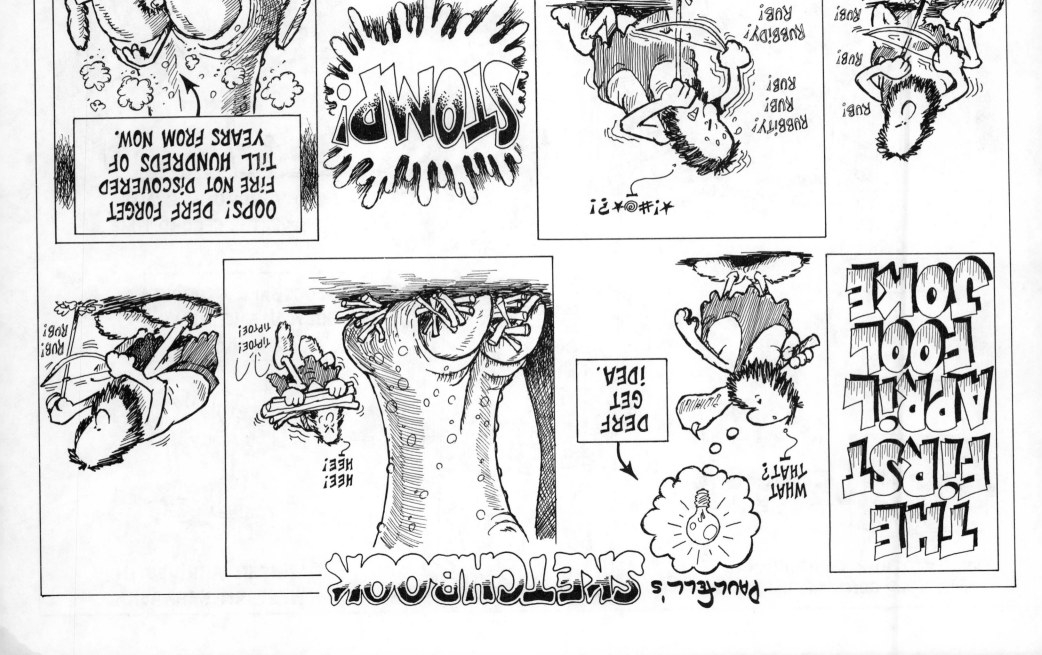

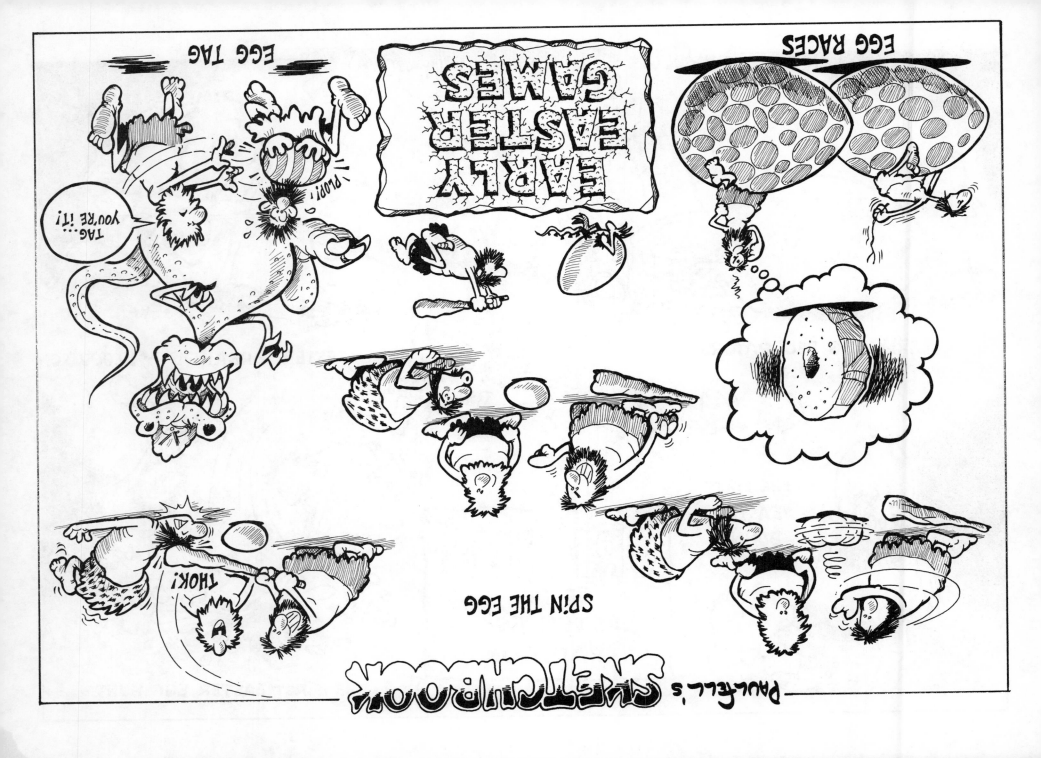

PAUL FELL's SKETCHBOOK

SUPPLIES FOR THE BACKYARD CHEF

1. PROPER FUEL

SUP-R CHARCOAL
STARTS EVENTUALLY

2. CHARCOAL STARTER

BIG CHEF

COME AND GET IT!

3. SUITABLE ATTIRE

4. THE RIGHT FIXIN'S...

MEAT FOR HIM TO GRILL

MEAT FOR THE FAMILY TO EAT

FIRE 911

ED'S CATERING 775-7000

POISON CONTROL 991-1100

5. COMMUNICATIONS

PAULFELL's SKETCHBOOK

LAST YEAR'S SWIMSUIT SHRANK.

11 HOT DOGS AND A GALLON OF POP IS TOO MUCH.

THE SUN IS MORE INTENSE ON WEEKENDS.

SACK RACES ARE FOR KIDS.

POISON IVY HAS THREE LEAVES.

MEMORIAL DAY MEMORIES...

SKUNKS LOOK JUST LIKE CATS.

PAULFELL's SKETCHBOOK

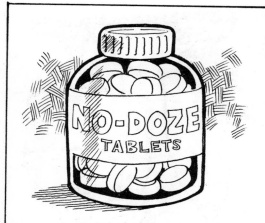

FOR THE NEW DOCTOR

FOR THE FATHER OF THE GRADUATE

PART-TIME JOB GUIDE

LIVING ON A LIMITED INCOME

FOR THE NEW TEACHER

FOR THE NEW CHEF

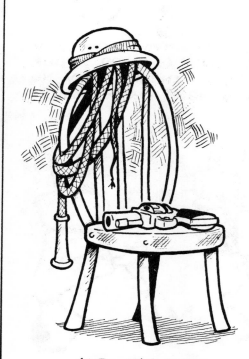

FOR THE NEW BABY SITTER

FOR THE NEW UMPIRE

EAR PLUGS

GRADUATION GIFTS

12 DOZ. ACME CLICHÉS

FOR THE NEW SPORTSCASTER

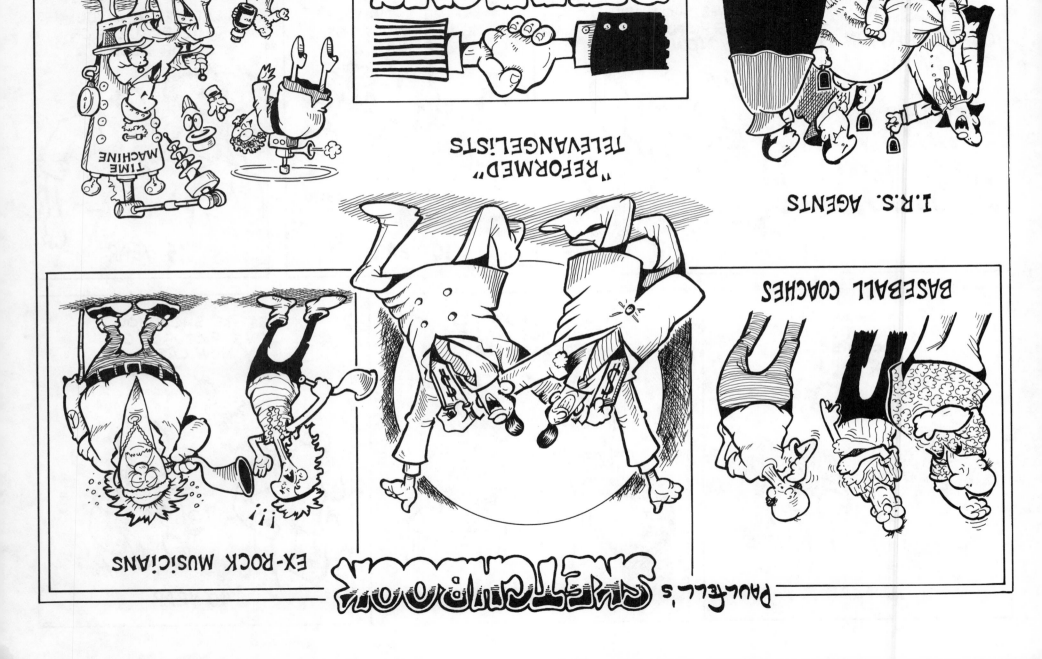

CREATURES OR KIDS!

WHY SOME FOLKS PREFER TO RAISE PETS INSTEAD OF CHILDREN

YOUR HAMSTER WON'T EVER NEED A WEDDING DRESS.

A HORSE WILL NEVER PESTER YOU FOR A $250 SKATEBOARD.

YOU WILL NEVER HAVE TO TEACH YOUR 16-YEAR-OLD CAT HOW TO DRIVE.

YOU'LL NEVER HAVE TO PUT YOUR DOG THROUGH COLLEGE.

FISH COMMUNICATE ALMOST AS WELL AS SOME TEENS.

PaulELL's SKETCHBOOK

A FEW
REASONS TO
APPRECIATE
NEBRASKA
SUMMERS

PAUL FELL's SKETCHBOOK

YOU FORGET ABOUT WIND CHILL.

THIS IS MUCH
BETTER.

SURE IS.

YOU GET TO GRILL OUT.

YOU NEVER HAVE TO
SHOVEL SNOW.

AWWW....
SHADDUP...!

YOU'LL HAVE SOMETHING TO BRAG
ABOUT DURING THE WINTER.

... AND IT GOT SO HOT IN JULY MY
MOTHER-IN-LAW MELTED.

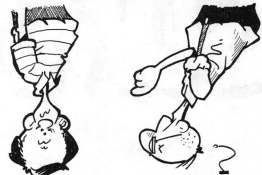

SUMMER JOB OPPORTUNITIES FOR YOUTH.

fRYeD egg
SAndwiches?

EGGS

BREAD

TWO, OVER
EASY...

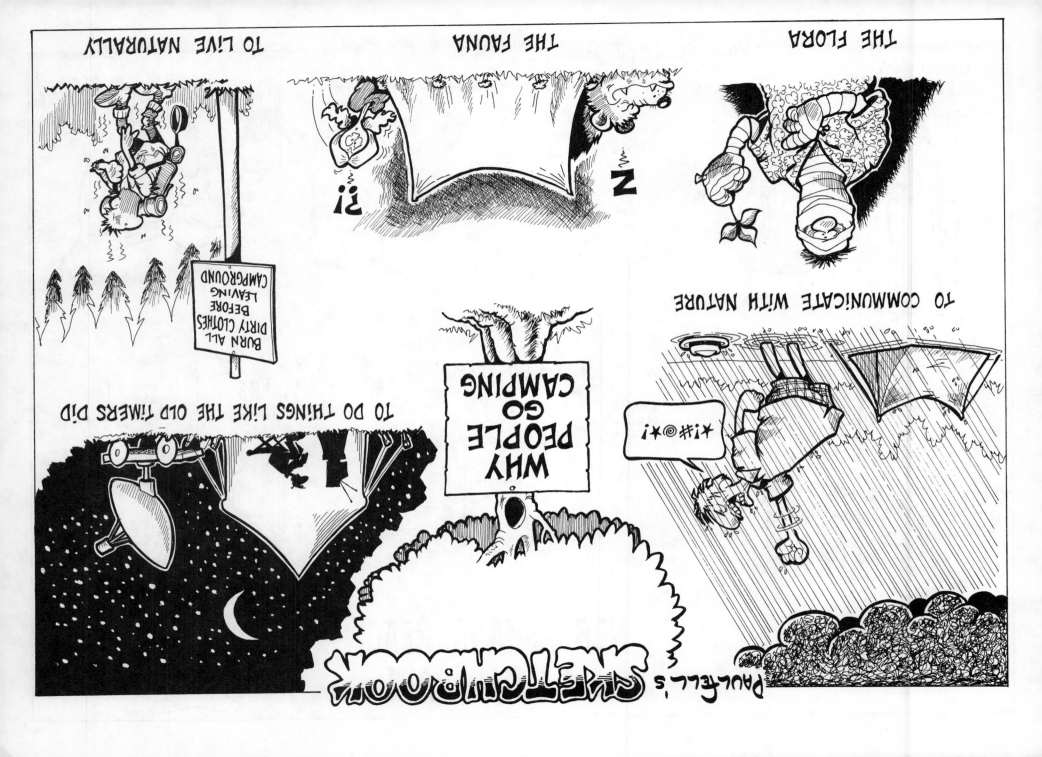

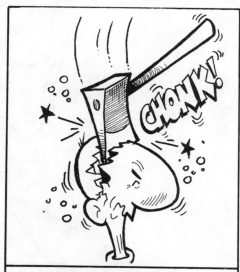

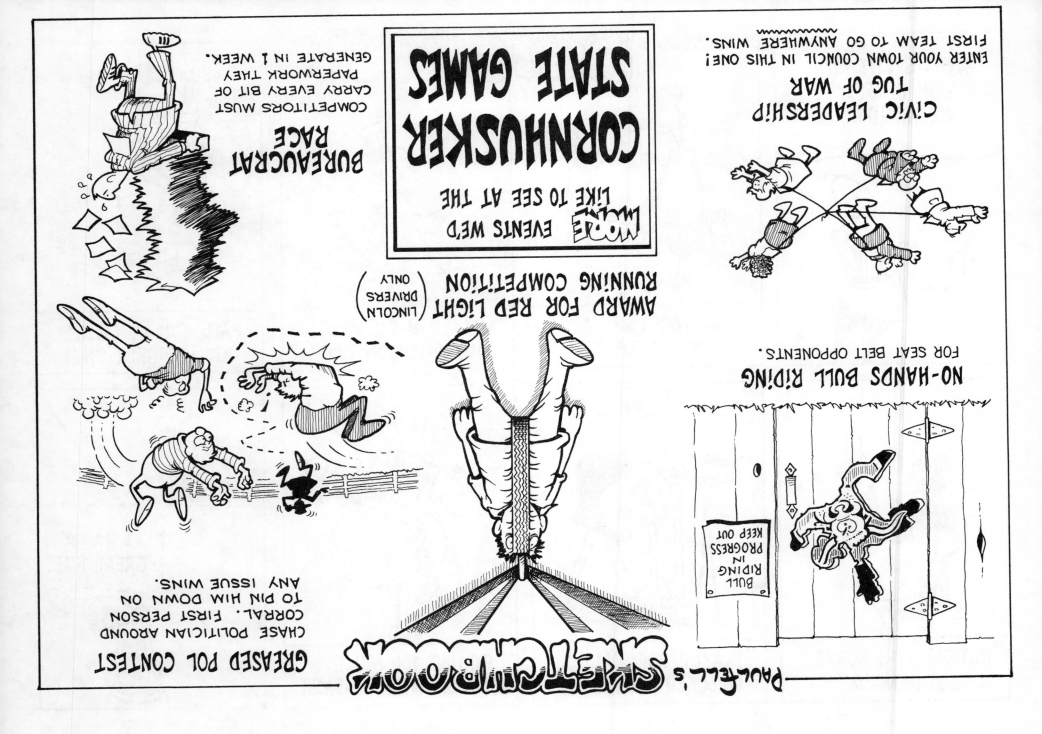

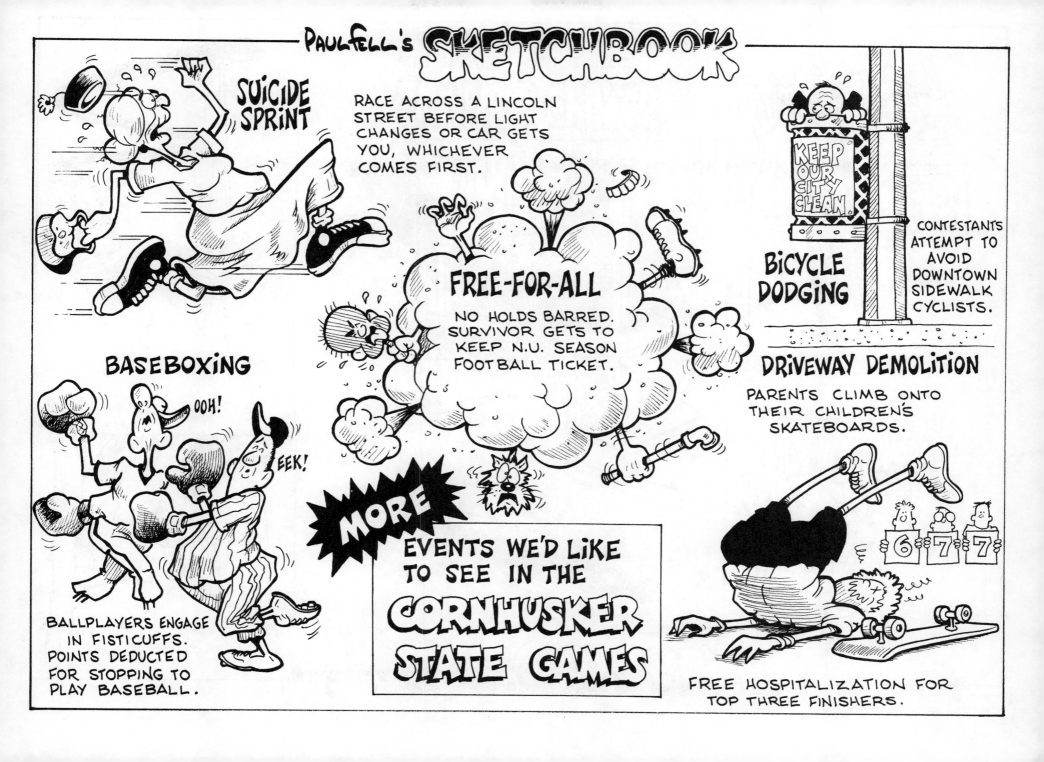

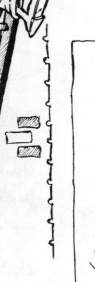

SUMMER CHORES
you never quite got
around to doing.

PAULELL's SKETCHBOOK

Paulfell's SKETCHBOOK

YOU BEGIN TO DREAD GOING TO WORK.

YOU WATCH THE CLOCK CONSTANTLY.

YOU SNAP AT YOUR CO-WORKERS.

GRRRRR!

HOW TO TELL WHEN YOU NEED A VACATION...

YOU CAN'T KEEP YOUR MIND ON BUSINESS.

YOU CONSIDER STOWING AWAY ON THE NEIGHBORS' R.V.

YOU THINK ABOUT SENDING THE KIDS TO CAMP.

CAMP LEJEUNE

Paul Fell's SKETCHBOOK

AAAGGH!
A BUG!
I SAW A BUG!

GO CAMPING WITH SOMEONE WHOSE IDEA OF ROUGHING IT IS TO GO TO A HOTEL AND NOT ORDER ROOM SERVICE.

SEE 5 STATES
IN 4 DAYS
WITH 6 KIDS

IN A NON-AIR CONDITIONED AUTOMOBILE.

GO ANYWHERE WITH A SPOUSE WHO GOES BERSERK AROUND ANY SIGN THAT SAYS "FACTORY OUTLET".

TAKING YOUR HUSBAND

TO VISIT YOUR PARENTS.

HOW TO LOSE YOUR MIND IN 1 WEEK OR LESS...

TAKING THE KIDS SOMEPLACE THEY KNOW IS EDUCATIONAL.

PAULFELL'S SKETCHBOOK

AT THIS POINT IN THE SUMMER, SOME TEENS WILL DO ANYTHING TO GET OUT OF THE HOUSE AND AVOID CHORES...

AND WE DO MEAN ANYTHING...!

WELCOME TO H.H.S. BAND CAMP

8 MI. TO GO

TOING!

FOUR...

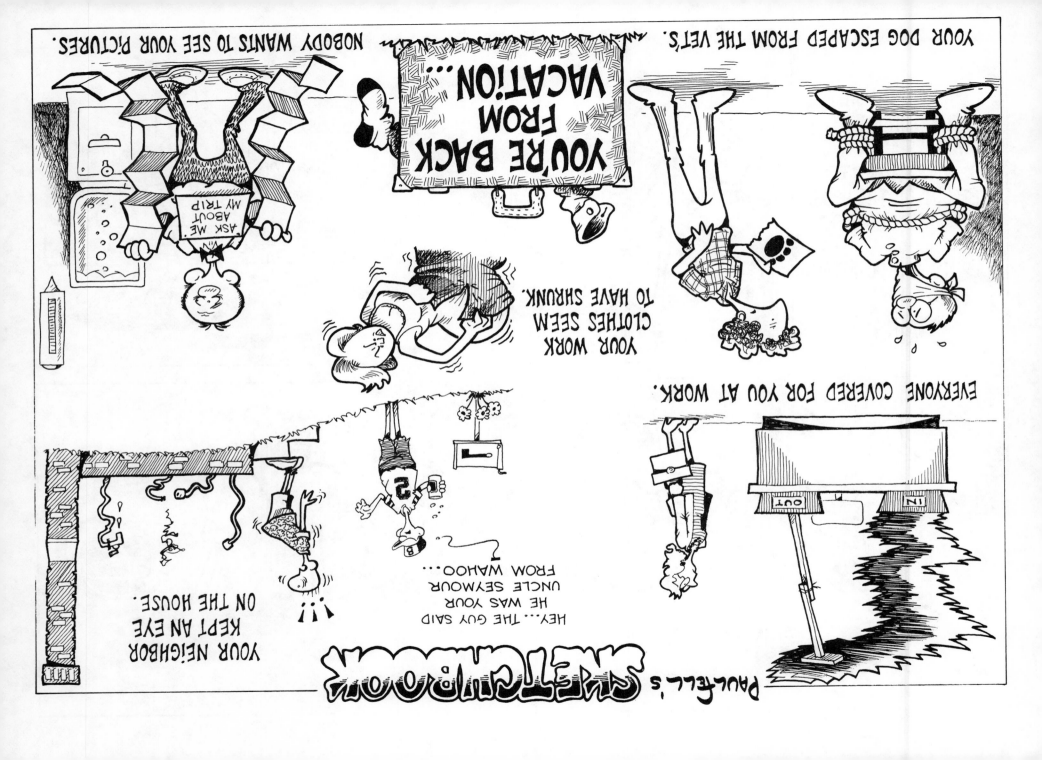

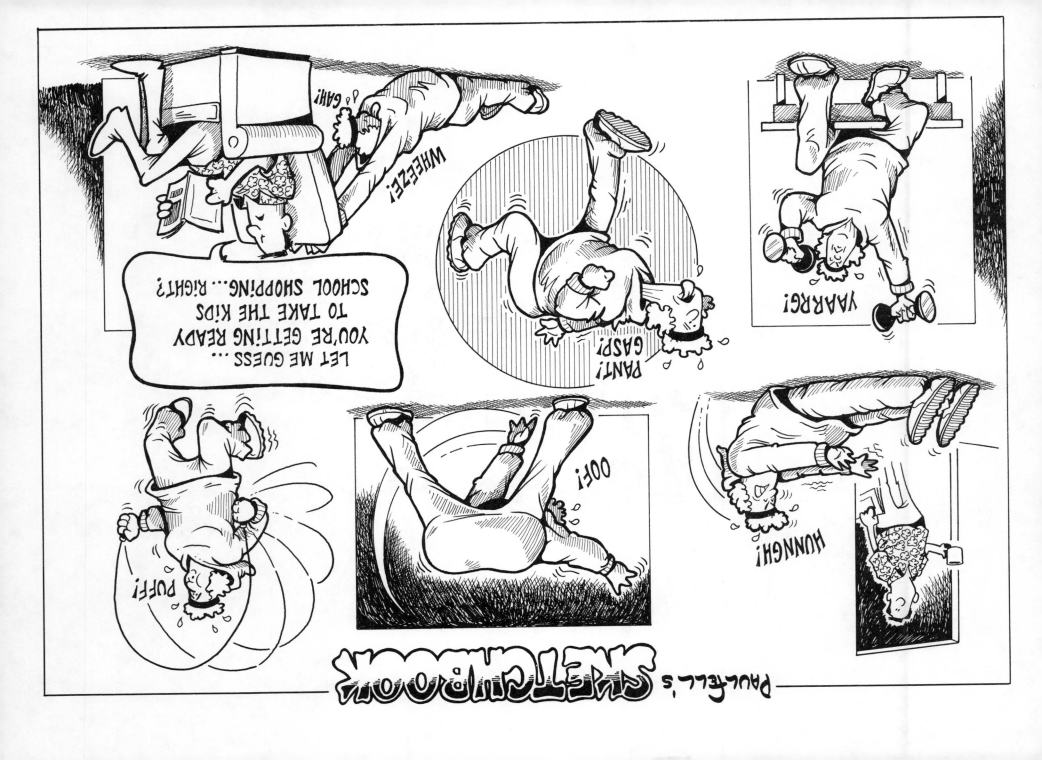

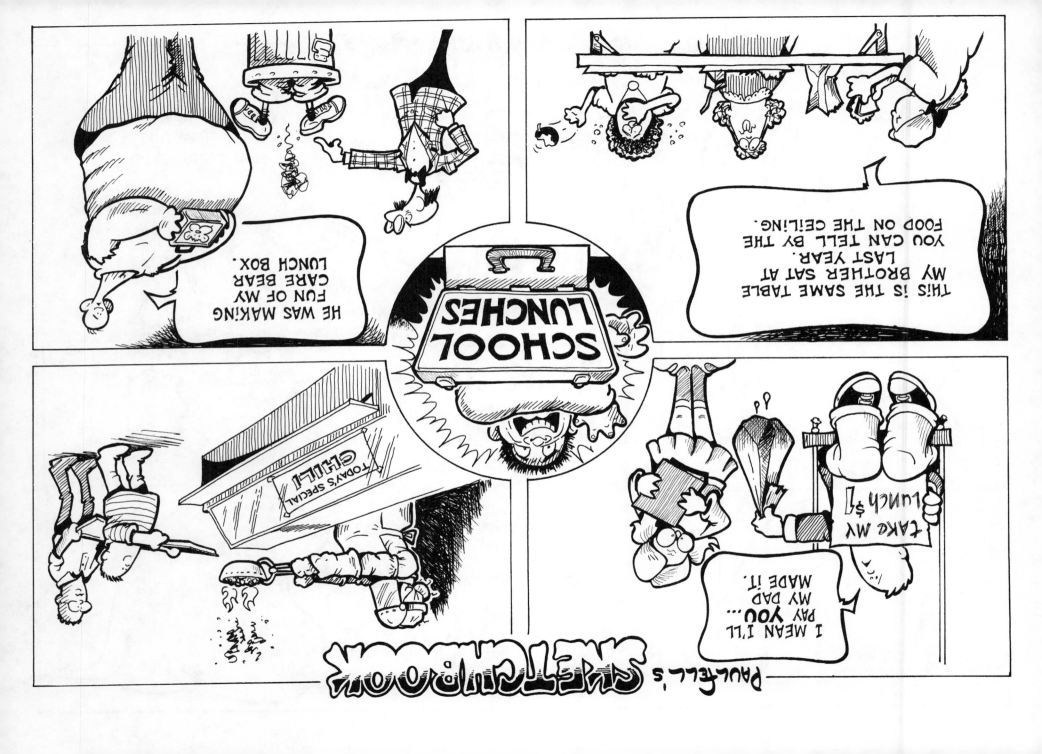

PAUL FELL'S SKETCHBOOK

FALL CHORE CHECKLIST

REPLACE FURNACE FILTERS

CLEAN CHIMNEY

CHECK WEATHER STRIPPING AROUND WINDOWS & DOORS

HANG STORM WINDOWS

CLEAN GUTTERS & DOWNSPOUTS

PAULFELL's **SKETCHBOOK**

PARENT-TEACHER CONFERENCE

WHAT YOUR CHILD'S TEACHER REALLY MEANS WHEN SHE SAYS:

"HE'S AGGRESSIVELY OUTGOING."

(THE LITTLE THUG BEAT UP 3 KIDS DURING RECESS LAST WEEK.)

"HAS UNUSUAL APTITUDE FOR HANDS-ON ACTIVITIES."

(WE CAUGHT HIM TRYING TO BUILD LAND MINES IN METAL SHOP.)

"UNUSUAL ATTENTION SPAN FOR A CHILD HIS AGE".

(30 SECONDS AND HE'S OFF TO LA-LA LAND.)

"WE'RE WORKING WITH HIM TO IMPROVE HIS SOCIAL SKILLS."

(IF HE DUNKS ICKY DOLAN IN THE TOILET ONCE MORE, HE'S OUTTA HERE.)

"WE WELCOME INCREASED PARENTAL INVOLVEMENT."

(HOW ABOUT A LITTLE HELP FROM YOUR END, HUH?)

"HIS PHYSICAL & ACADEMIC DEVELOPMENT ARE ON DIFFERENT LEVELS."

(THESE DAYS YOU DON'T FIND MANY 4th. GRADERS OLD ENOUGH TO DRIVE.)

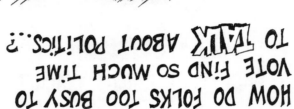

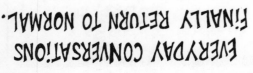

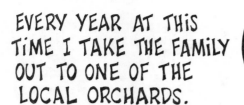

EVERY YEAR AT THIS TIME I TAKE THE FAMILY OUT TO ONE OF THE LOCAL ORCHARDS.

THE WIFE AND I ENJOY THE DRIVE AND THE KIDS LOVE GETTING OUT IN THE COUNTRY.

EVERYONE GETS SO EXCITED ABOUT THE NICE FALL WEATHER AND THOSE FRESH, DELICIOUS APPLES...

... THAT WE ALWAYS BUY PLENTY TO TAKE HOME.

(SIGH..!) ONLY 33½ BUSHELS TO GO...

PAULFELL's SKETCHBOOK

SHOW A LITTLE MORE RESTRAINT IN THE BUFFET LINE.

AFTER-THANKSGIVING PROMISES

BEFORE YOU ARGUE POLITICS AGAIN WITH YOUR WIFE'S MOTHER, RECALL HOW COLD AND LONELY DINNER OUT ON THE BACK STEPS WAS.

AVOID PHILOSOPHICAL DISAGREEMENTS WITH YOUR VEGETARIAN SISTER-IN-LAW.

TRY NOT TO DOZE OFF AFTER DINNER.

LOSE 15 POUNDS BY CHRISTMAS*

AUGGHH!

* SO WE CAN DO IT ALL OVER AGAIN.

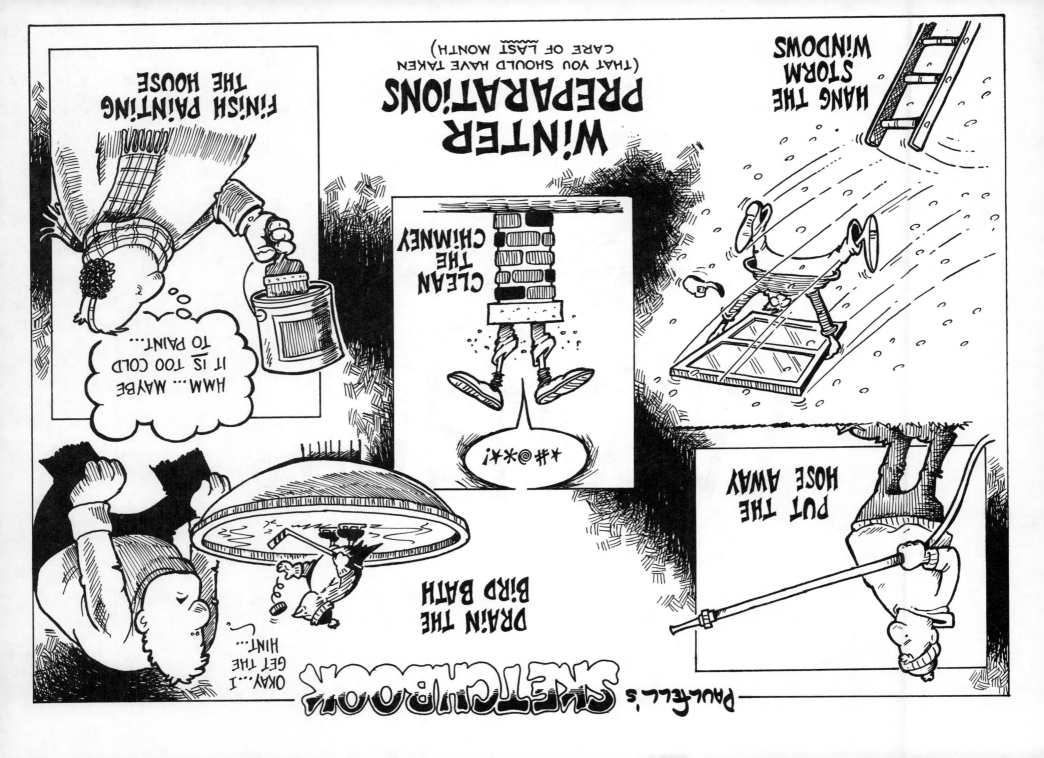

Paul Fell's SKETCHBOOK

EVERY CAR SEEMS TO HAVE A TREE GROWING OUT OF IT.

EACH SENTENCE YOUR KID UTTERS SEEMS TO BEGIN WITH "I WANT..."

DO NOT OPEN UNTIL XMAS

I WENT IN TO BUY SOME PAINT AND TOOK A WRONG TURN...

CRAZED PACKS OF MOTHERS RAMPAGE THROUGH DISCOUNT STORE TOY DEPARTMENTS.

THE WEATHER TURNS MORE SEASONAL. QUICKLY.

SIGNS OF CHRISTMAS

ADVERTISING INCREASES FOR JEWELRY THAT COSTS MORE THAN YOUR HOUSE.

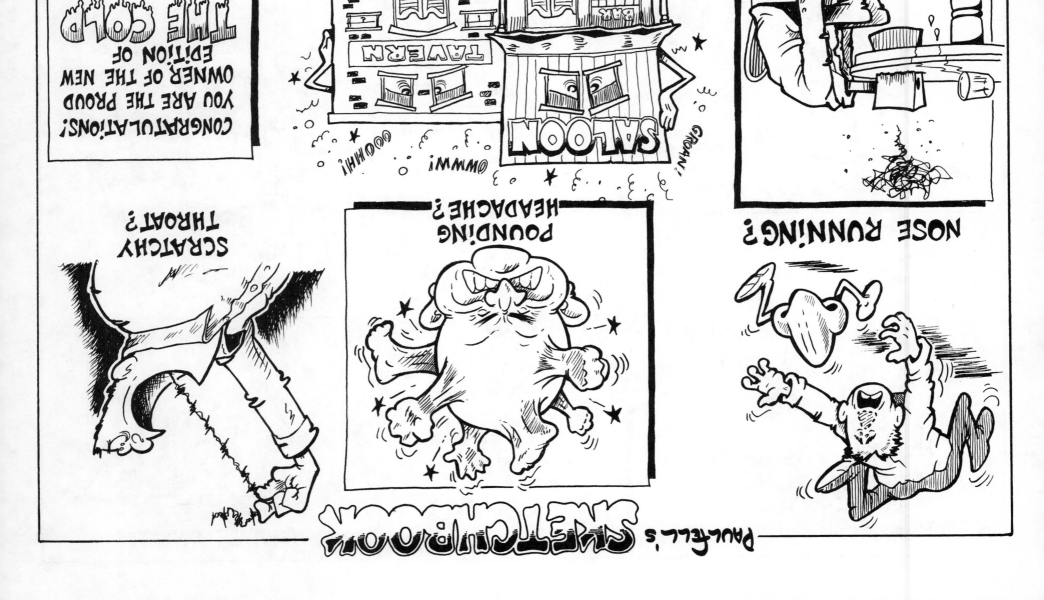

PAULFELL's SKETCHBOOK

SCHEDULE A SLUMBER PARTY IN THE DEN.

INVITE YOUR MOTHER FOR A LONG VISIT.

HOW TO DRIVE HIM CRAZY DURING THE NEW YEAR'S BOWL GAMES...

TAKE HIM OUT FOR A WALK.

"FORGET" TO PAY THE CABLE T.V. BILL.

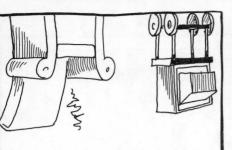

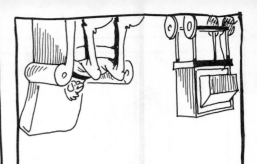

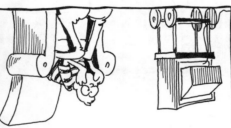

WELL, I'LL BE....
IT WORKED.

GAH!

SPING!

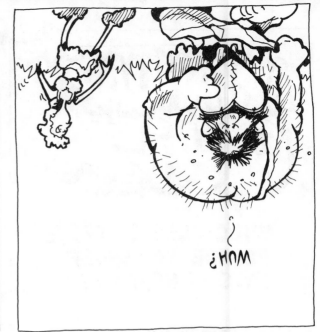

WUH?

LOOK HERE...
I MADE THIS
FOR YOU.

UH?

IF YOU THINK I'M
GONNA LET YOU
BONK ME ON THE
HEAD & DRAG ME
OFF TO YOUR CAVE,
GUESS AGAIN,
BUSTER!!

THE FIRST
VALENTINE

PaulELL's SKETCHBOOK

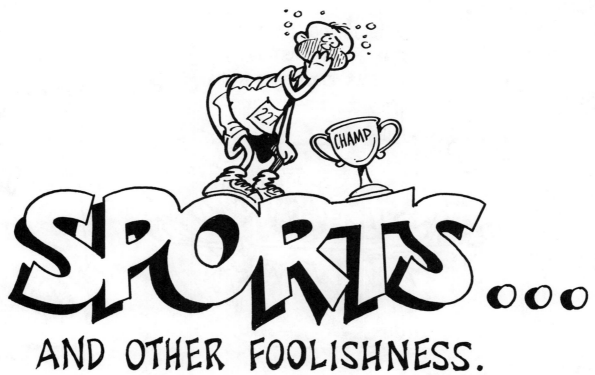

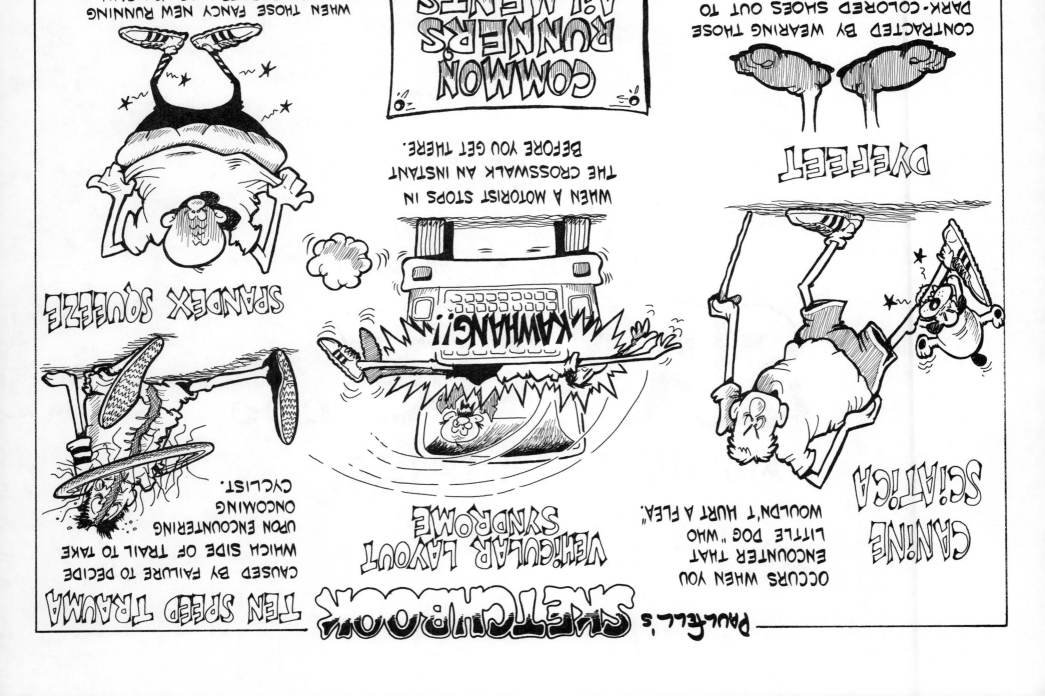

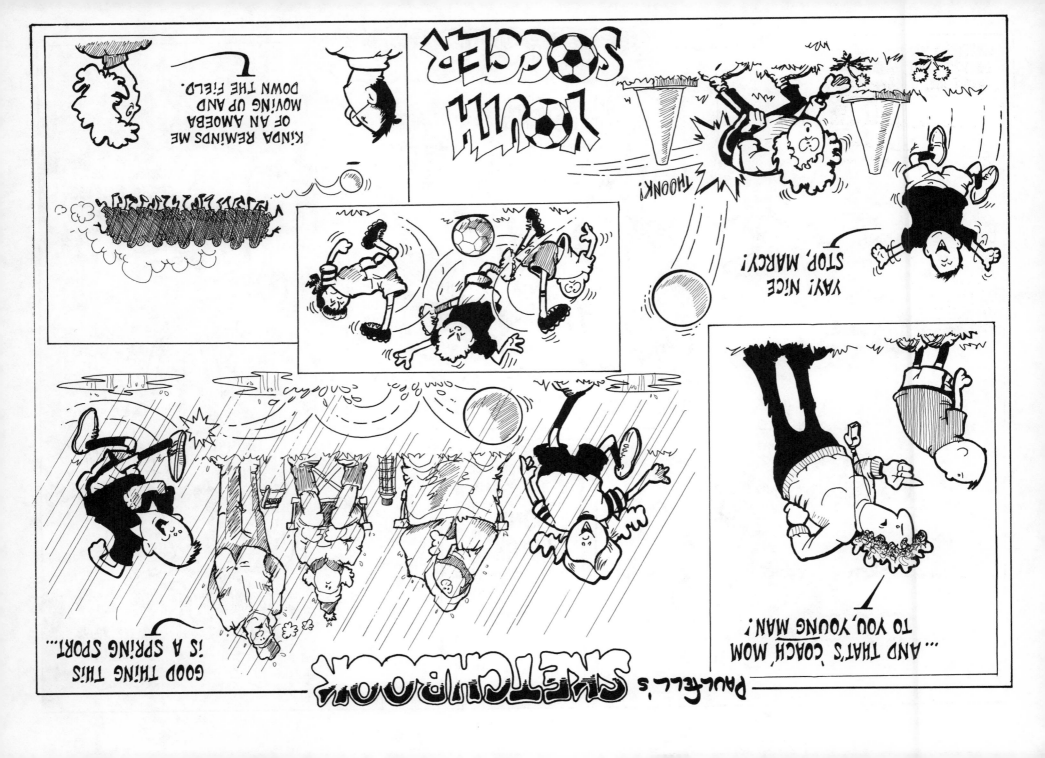

O, FEARLESS LEADER, I COME FROM OBSERVING THE ALIENS AND FIND THEM TO BE VERY STRANGE BEINGS INDEED...

THEY GATHER INDOORS IN LARGE GROUPS AND INGEST MASS QUANTITIES OF ALL SORTS OF GREASY SUBSTANCES...

THEY MAKE A GREAT COMMOTION BY JUMPING ABOUT, CHANTING, AND WAVING SIGNS I WAS UNABLE TO DECIPHER...

GROUPS OF THEM SHARE A PREFERENCE FOR CERTAIN COLORS, AND MANY PAINT THEIR FACES OR DON BIZARRE HEADGEAR...

ALL OF THIS ACTIVITY SEEMS TO CENTER ON A SMALL GROUP WHO RUN BACK AND FORTH IN THEIR UNDERWEAR CHASING A BOUNCING SPHERE..!

PLEASE, O, GREAT ONE... GRANT ME A VACATION..! (GASP!)

REMIND ME NOT TO SEND ANY MORE EXPEDITIONS TO EARTH UNTIL BASKETBALL SEASON IS OVER.

PLOP!

PAULFELL's SKETCHBOOK

ATHLETIC SHOES

WHAT'S THE DIFFERENCE BETWEEN JOGGING SHOES AND RUNNING SHOES..?

ABOUT 75 BUCKS.

AIR BORDENS

I WANTED TO SEE HOW FAR I COULD PUMP UP MY NEW SHOES.

TAKE ONE SHORT KID WHO CAN'T JUMP...

ADD A $100+ PAIR OF SNEAKERS...

AND...

YOU GET ONE SHORT KID WHO STILL CAN'T JUMP BUT LOOKS GOOD TRYING.

WHERE THE FIRST THING YOU LEARN IN GEOGRAPHY IS THE LOCATION OF THE STATES IN THE BIG 8 CONFERENCE.

WHERE HATING THE SOONERS JUST ISN'T THE SAME SINCE BARRY SWITZER QUIT.

WHERE YOU ENJOY THE CHANGING SEASONS... TWO-A-DAYS, REGULAR SEASON, BOWL GAMES, SPRING BALL.

WHERE THIS KIND OF SIGNAL OUTSIDE MEMORIAL STADIUM MEANS "LET'S MAKE A DEAL"...

WELCOME to FOOTBALL COUNTRY

WHERE HARDLY ANYONE CAN REMEMBER THE LAST TIME THE CORNHUSKERS DIDN'T GET AN INVITATION TO A POST-SEASON BOWL GAME.

WHERE EVERYONE'S IDEA OF A TRICK PLAY IS A FORWARD PASS.

PAULFELL's SKETCHBOOK

YOU TRY TO JUMP UP TO TOUCH THE RIM AND GET A NOSEBLEED.

YOU FIND IT'S TOO DANGEROUS TO PLAY VOLLEYBALL WITH YOUR 7th. GRADE DAUGHTER.

WHENEVER YOU SEE JOGGERS YOUR KNEES ACHE.

AAAAAHH!

YOU HURT YOURSELF WHEN YOU TRY TO GET ON YOUR BIKE.

HOW TO TELL WHEN YOU'VE BECOME AN EX- SPORTS "SUPERSTAR"...

GASP! SNORT! GAH!

THE WARM-UP AND COOL-DOWN PORTION OF YOUR WORKOUT BECOMES THE ONLY PART YOU CAN DO.

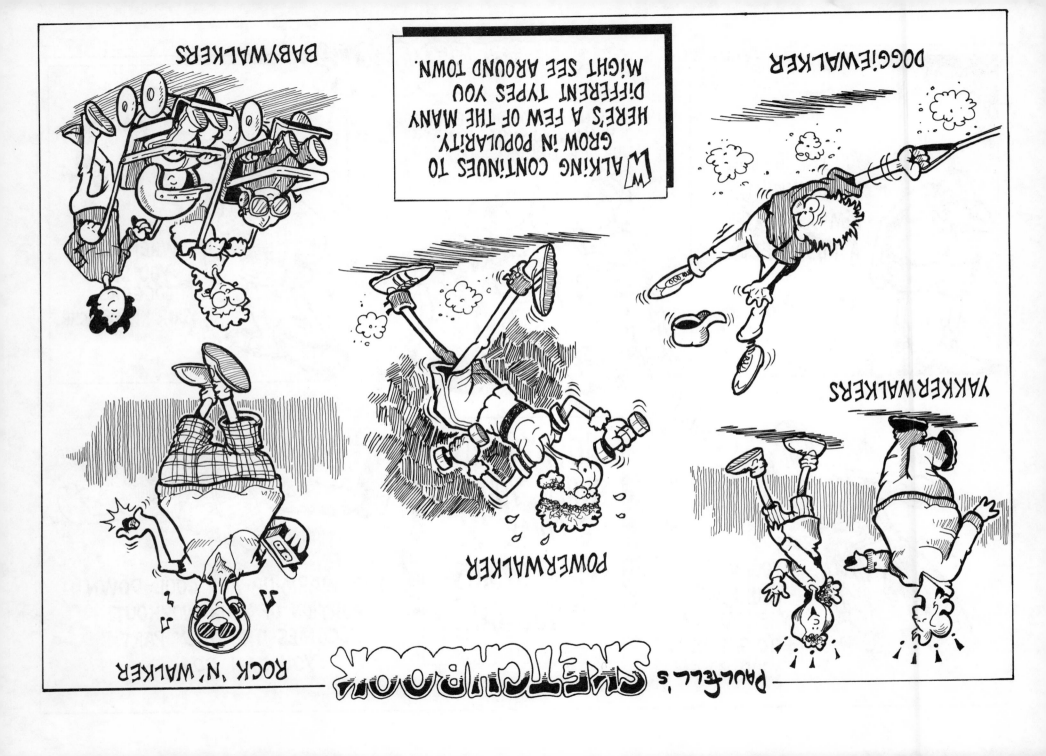

PAULFELL's SKETCHBOOK

ALONG SHERIDAN BLVD.

DOWNTOWN

AT HOLMES LAKE

20th. STREET & HWY 2

WALKERS

YAK! YAK!

AROUND FOX HOLLOW

NEAR 70th & VAN DORN

40th. & NORMAL

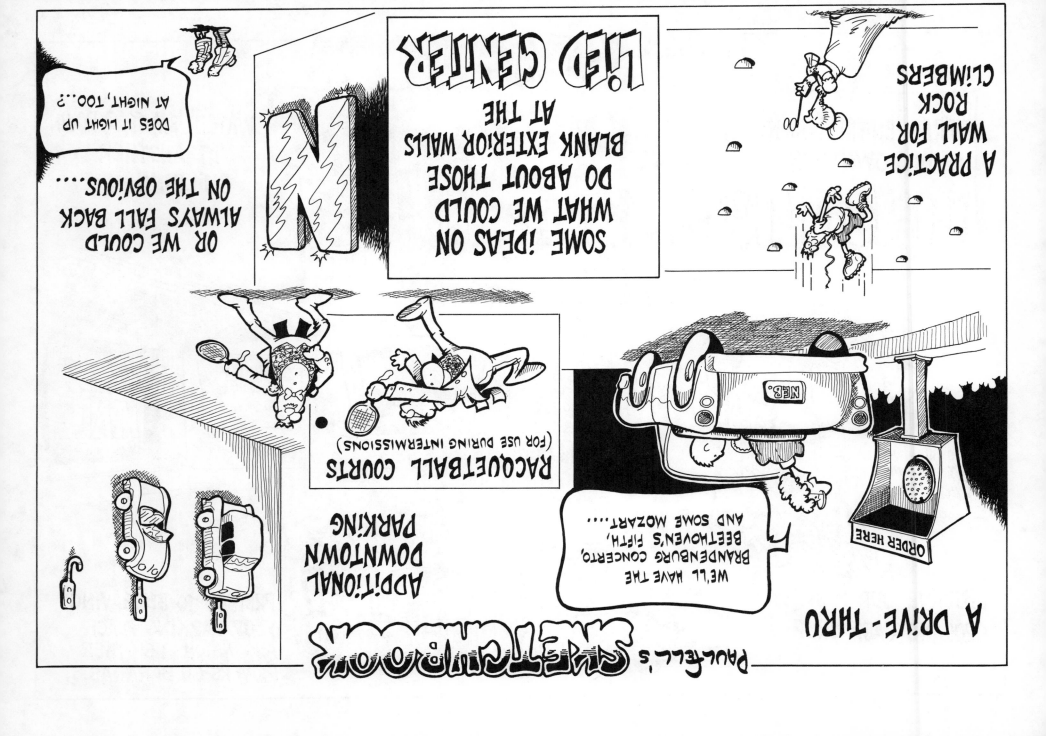

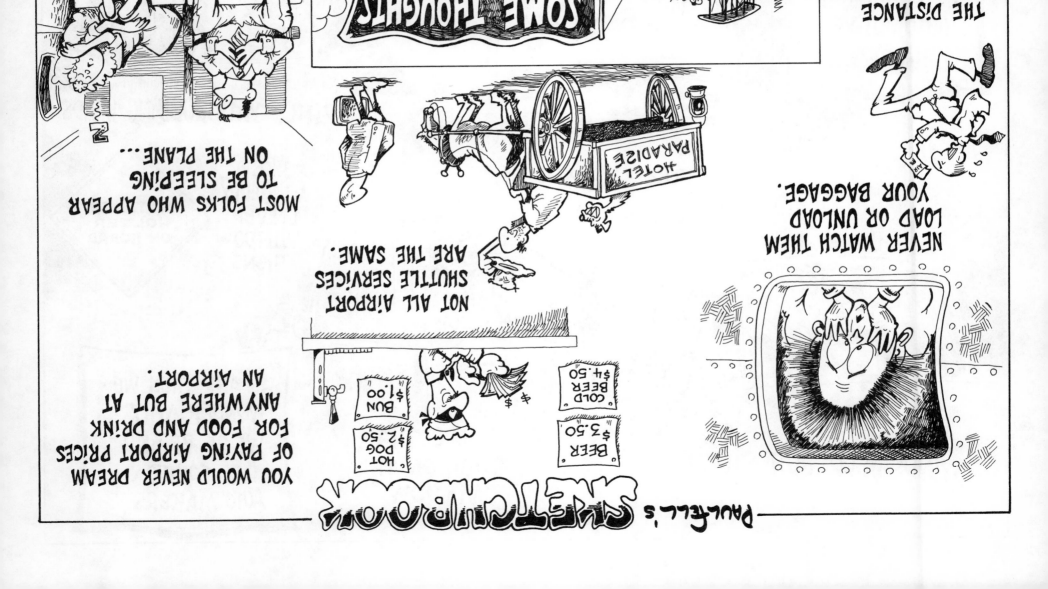

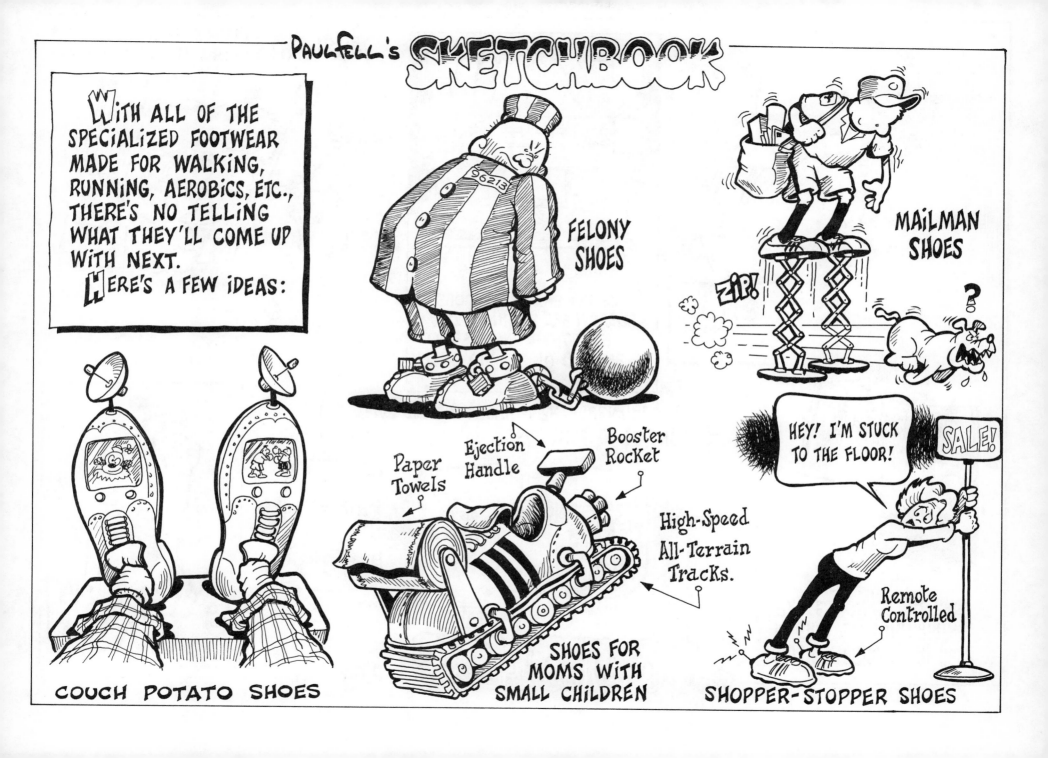

Paulfell's SKETCHBOOK

GETTING FRIENDS TO HELP IS CHEAPER THAN HIRING PROFESSIONAL MOVERS. SOMETIMES.

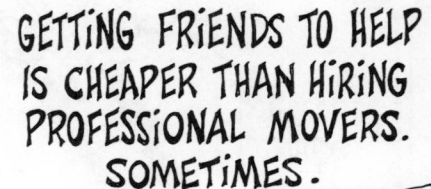

MOVING DAY

THIS END UP

Rx TRANQUILIZERS

PEPTO BLASTO

ACME GLUE

WHEN MOVING WITH THE ASSISTANCE OF FRIENDS THE ITEMS SHOWN ABOVE ARE ESSENTIAL.

YEE-HAH!

FRAGILE

IT IS UNWISE TO CHANGE ONE'S MIND TOO OFTEN ABOUT WHERE THE MOVERS SHOULD SET THE PIANO.

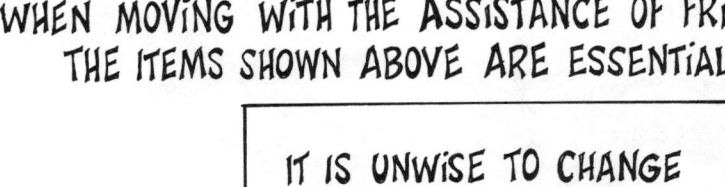

OKAY... LET 'ER GO!

DON'T BREAK OUT THE BEER UNTIL YOUR VOLUNTEER HELP FINISHES THE MOVE.